Optimism and Self-Confidence

CAUSES & EFFECTS OF EMOTIONS

CAUSES & EFFECTS OF EMOTIONS

Optimism and Self-Confidence

Z.B. Hill

Mason Crest

Mason Crest
450 Parkway Drive, Suite D
Broomall, PA 19008
www.masoncrest.com

Printed and bound in the United States of America.

First printing
9 8 7 6 5 4 3 2 1

Series ISBN: 978-1-4222-3067-1
ISBN: 978-1-4222-3076-3
ebook ISBN: 978-1-4222-8769-9

The Library of Congress has cataloged the
hardcopy format(s) as follows:
        Library of Congress Cataloging-in-Publication Data

Hill, Z. B.
  Optimism and self-confidence / Z.B. Hill.
     pages cm. — (Causes & effects of emotions)
  Audience: Age 12+
  Audience: Grade 7 to 8.
  ISBN 978-1-4222-3076-3 (hardback) — ISBN 978-1-4222-3067-1 (series)
— ISBN 978-1-4222-8769-9 (ebook) 1. Optimism—Juvenile literature. 2.
Self-confidence in adolescence—Juvenile literature. I. Title.
  BF698.35.O57H55 2015
  155.2'32—dc23
                                        2014004382

CONTENTS

KEY ICONS TO LOOK FOR:

Text-Dependent Questions: These questions send the reader back to the text for more careful attention to the evidence presented there.

Words to Understand: These words with their easy-to-understand definitions will increase the reader's understanding of the text, while building vocabulary skills.

Series Glossary of Key Terms: This back-of-the book glossary contains terminology used throughout this series. Words found here increase the reader's ability to read and comprehend higher-level books and articles in this field.

Research Projects: Readers are pointed toward areas of further inquiry connected to each chapter. Suggestions are provided for projects that encourage deeper research and analysis.

Sidebars: This boxed material within the main text allows readers to build knowledge, gain insights, explore possibilities, and broaden their perspectives by weaving together additional information to provide realistic and holistic perspectives.

INTRODUCTION

The journey of self-discovery for young adults can be a passage that includes times of introspection as well joyful experiences. It can also be a complicated route filled with confusing road signs and hazards along the way. The choices teens make will have lifelong impacts. From early romantic relationships to complex feelings of anxiousness, loneliness, and compassion, this series of books is designed specifically for young adults, tackling many of the challenges facing them as they navigate the social and emotional world around and within them. Each chapter explores the social emotional pitfalls and triumphs of young adults, using stories in which readers will see themselves reflected.

Adolescents encounter compound issues today in home, school, and community. Many young adults may feel ill equipped to identify and manage the broad range of emotions they experience as their minds and bodies change and grow. They face many adult problems without the knowledge and tools needed to find satisfactory solutions. Where do they fit in? Why are they afraid? Do others feel as lonely and lost as they do? How do they handle the emotions that can engulf them when a friend betrays them or they fail to make the grade? These are all important questions that young adults may face. Young adults need guidance to pilot their way through changing feelings that are influenced by peers, family relationships, and an ever-changing world. They need to know that they share common strengths and pressures with their peers. Realizing they are not alone with their questions can help them develop important attributes of resilience and hope.

The books in this series skillfully capture young people's everyday, real-life emotional journeys and provides practical and meaningful information that can offer hope to all who read them.

It covers topics that teens may be hesitant to discuss with others, giving them a context for their own feelings and relationships. It is an essential tool to help young adults understand themselves and their place in the world around them—and a valuable asset for teachers and counselors working to help young people become healthy, confident, and compassionate members of our society.

Cindy Croft, M.A.Ed
Director of the Center for Inclusive Child Care at Concordia University

Words to Understand

perspectives: Points of view; ways to approach something.
negative: Seeing mainly the downside of something.
positive: Seeing mainly the upside.
challenges: Difficult moments that test your abilities in some
  way.
depressed: Having a strong feeling of sadness and hopelessness, often
  for a long time.
researched: Did tests and studies to try to learn more about something.
psychologists: Experts on the human mind and emotions.
aberration: An unusual or strange result.

ONE

WHAT ARE OPTIMISM & SELF-CONFIDENCE?

On a Saturday morning, Lisa and her sister Amy both get out of bed and look out their bedroom window. The sky is covered with clouds, and Amy groans. "Oh no, it's going to rain! They'll have to cancel the softball game today."

Lisa shakes her head. "No, they won't. It's just cloudy. It's not raining. Besides, the game isn't for another three hours. By then maybe the sun will have come out."

Two hours later, as the two sisters get dressed in their uniforms, the sun hasn't come out, but it's not raining either. "See," Lisa says, "I told you they wouldn't have to cancel the game."

As the girls' mom drives them to softball field, Amy's cell phone rings. It's their friend Jessica, saying she's come down with a stomach virus and she's not going to be able to play today.

As Amy puts her phone back in her backpack, she's clearly

For the optimist everything looks possible—while to the pessimist, challenges may seem too great to overcome.

upset. "Now we're sure to lose! Without Jessica we don't have a chance. She's our best pitcher."

Lisa just smiles. "We'll be fine. You're as good as at pitching as Jessica, Amy."

Amy scowls and shakes her head. "No, I'm not! I always get nervous and then I mess up. I know we're going to lose. I wish it *had* rained and they'd cancelled the game. At least then we wouldn't have had to get slaughtered by the other team."

Lisa gives her sister a little pat. "Well, I'm a pretty good pitcher too, you know. And we've got a lot of good players on our team. I know we can play a good game."

"How can you be so calm?" Amy wails. "Everything is going wrong."

But Lisa shakes her head. "No, it isn't. Jessica got sick, but it isn't the end of the world."

Their mother parks the car and the sisters grab their gloves and get out. "I wish I'd just stayed home," Amy whispers to Lisa as they turn toward the field. "I'm so nervous I feel like I'm going to be sick too. I just know we're going to lose."

Lisa puts her arm around her sister's shoulders. "Don't worry," she tells Amy. "We've practiced hard. We're good players, and we've got a good team. We've got a good coach. It's going to be fun!"

A few hours later, the two sisters are back home, telling their father about the game. "It was a great game," Lisa says. "We won in the final inning. We were fantastic!"

Amy sighs. "We just got lucky. We almost lost."

DIFFERENT OUTLOOKS ON LIFE

These two sisters have very different *perspectives*. Amy's outlook is *negative*, but Lisa's is *positive*. Amy is a pessimist, while Lisa is an optimist. Lisa has healthy self-confidence, but Amy doubts her own abilities.

An optimist is someone who believes that the world is basically a good place where good things happen more often than not. When things go wrong, the optimist believes that everything will work out all right in the end. He's full of hope. If he looks at a glass of water that's half empty and half full, he focuses on the half that's full. And when life gives him lemons, he makes lemonade. He's a lot like Lisa.

A pessimist is just the opposite. He expects bad things to happen. Even when something good does happen, the pessimist thinks it won't be enough to prevent disaster. He assumes that the world is a bad place that's full of disappointment and failure. So when someone hands him that same glass of water that the optimist was looking at, the pessimist complains that the glass is half empty. When life gives him lemons, he throws up his hands and gives up. He and Amy have a lot in common.

Optimists aren't merely cheerful, happy people, while pessimists are gloomy and sad. It goes a step or two further than that.

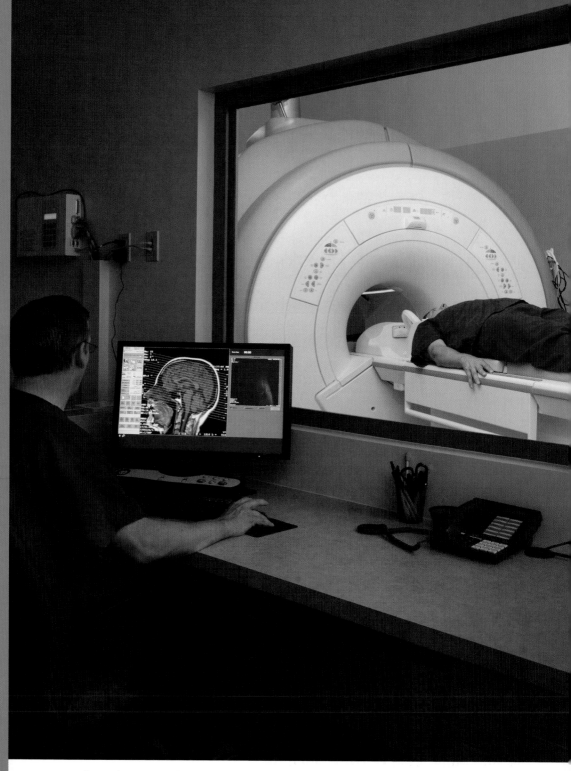

OPTIMISM AND SELF-CONFIDENCE

MRIs allow doctors to look inside a person's brain to see what is happening there. For the person being examined, it's a painless procedure.

Make Connections

Magnetic resonance imaging (MRI) is a test that uses a magnetic field and pulses of radio wave energy to make pictures of organs and structures inside the body. For an MRI test, the area of the body being studied is placed inside a special machine that contains a strong magnet. Pictures from an MRI scan are digital images that can be saved and stored on a computer for more study.

Optimists also are more likely to have self-confidence, while pessimists often doubt their own abilities. People with self-confidence believe in themselves. Like Lisa, they recognize the things they are good at, and they trust themselves to do a good job when they give something their best efforts. They're not afraid to try something new, and they handle *challenges* as they come along. People who lack self-confidence, however, don't believe in themselves. Like Amy, they're scared of failing.

Optimism and self-confidence are positive emotions. People who are optimistic and self-confident feel happier in general. They're less likely to be *depressed*. It may seem like they're lucky.

But emotions like optimism and self-confidence aren't merely good luck.

EMOTIONS

Our emotions are the feelings inside our minds. We've been experiencing them our entire life, ever since we were babies. Sometimes we feel happy, and sometimes we feel sad; sometime we feel angry, sometimes we're scared, and sometimes we are bored. All these feelings come and go inside us. We may feel as though we have little control over them.

We may also feel as though our inside feelings are telling us about outside reality. So when we feel sad, for example, we

Researchers are learning more and more about the chemicals inside our brains that produce emotions.

may believe that the world really is a gloomy place where bad things happen. We believe our sadness tells us something about the outside the world. Really, though, our sadness only tells us about ourselves. It may have been triggered by something that happened in the outside world, but the feeling itself is inside our brains. Chemicals inside our brains cause the feeling of sadness. Our brain cells are what create the different emotions we experiences, including optimism and self-confidence.

Scientists have *researched* human emotions. They've done experiments on brain cells. They've used machines like MRIs to actually look inside people's brains and see what's going on in there.

They've found out that what seem like emotional feelings to us are really changes taking place in our brains. Different kinds of events trigger different responses inside of human beings' brains, and we've learned to give those responses labels—like "happiness," "love," "anger," and "fear."

These responses inside your brain do important jobs. They direct your attention toward things that are important. When something makes you happy, for example, your brain says, "Notice this! Try to get more of this in your life!" Or when something scares you, the reaction in your brains tells you, "Be careful!"

When you were a young child, you learned from your emotions. You learned what makes you happy and what makes you sad, what scares you and what makes you laugh. You learned to change your behavior in response. Positive emotions—like joy and excitement and optimism—give you the energy you need to be creative and do amazing things. Negative feelings—like grief and pessimism and fear—aren't all bad either. They can also do important jobs in your life. They can teach you to stay way from things that might hurt you.

Some emotions—like happiness and sadness—are fairly simple. Even very young children can understand these feelings. Others are more complicated. Emotions like optimism and self-confidence are complex feelings.

OPTIMISM

Psychologists have discovered a few things about optimism. By studying people who experience this emotion much of the time, psychologists have found some things these people all have in common.

Optimists don't only *believe* that they'll do well; they often actually do succeed, more often, in fact, than, pessimists do. Experts have found that optimism and success go hand-in-hand. Dr. Martin Seligman, a psychologist who has spent much of his life studying optimists, reports that all optimists look at problems the same way.

Optimists' positive attitudes can help them to achieve their goals.

First, they believe that problems don't last forever. When an optimistic person like Lisa runs into something bad—like cloudy skies or a team member getting sick—she believes it's a temporary setback. Pessimists like Amy, however, believe that the smallest problem is the kiss of doom.

Second, optimists believe that problems are pretty small in the grand scheme of things. They know that that cloudy days will come, but they believe that, overall, life is good—and no cloudy day can ruin the entire big picture of life that they carry in their minds.

And last, according to Dr. Seligman, optimists take credit for the victories that come along, while they blame defeats on circumstances beyond their control. When an optimist like Lisa wins a softball game, she takes credit for it. She claims hard work and skill as the reason for the victory. A pessimist like Amy, however, sees as it as a one-time *aberration*, something that's not likely to happen next time. If their team had lost instead of won, Lisa would have most likely said, "Oh well, we had some things go

Make Connections

Scientists believe that evolution gave human beings the emotions we feel today. Our prehistoric ancestors who had these reactions inside their brains lived longer than their companions who lacked these reactions. They avoided danger better. Because they lived longer, they were able to have children—and they passed along this trait to their children, who in turn passed it along to their children. Emotions help early humans cope with the world around them. They were survival mechanisms that helped the human race survive.

wrong today, but we'll do better next time." Lisa would practice even harder before the next game. Amy, however, would use the defeat as evidence that their team will lose the next game too. "We might as well give up," she might say when it came time for practice. "What's the point? We're just going to lose like we did last time."

Optimists' and pessimists' emotions shape reality. Because optimists and pessimists feel a certain way, they act a certain way—and their actions often lead to the very thing they were expecting, either success or defeat, depending on their outlooks. Alan Loy McGinnis, author of *The Power of Optimism*, studied the biographies of over a thousand famous people and found that they all had some things in common. Here are a few:

- Optimists look for partial solutions. They don't think success depends on all or nothing. They're open to taking small steps that could lead to success.
- Optimists use their imaginations to picture success. They play imaginary movies in their heads of what success will look like. (Successful athletes use this same technique.)
- Optimists believe that no matter what their skills are today,

Research Project

Find out more what experts think about optimism. Using the library and the Internet, research either Martin Seligman or Alan Loy McGinnis. See if you can find the answers to the following questions:

- What got the person interested in optimism?
- What steps did he take to find out more about optimism?
- What are the most important things he found out about optimism?
- Why is his work important?

Write a paragraph to answer each question.

they can improve them. They believe their personal best is yet to come, and they have confidence in their ability to grow.

This last trait points to the way optimism and self-confidence are linked together. Optimists are more successful in life—and successful people are more self-confident. They take action, even when they are not sure of the outcome. They have the confidence to take on challenges.

SELF-CONFIDENCE

A person with self-confidence has learned to trust himself. He recognizes his own skills, and he knows how to use them. Throughout his life, his parents, teachers, and friends have probably helped him believe in himself.

Having other people believe in us is an important part of self-confidence. If a person has been criticized by everyone around

Text-Dependent Questions

1. In the story about Amy and Lisa, give three examples from the text that show which sister is a pessimist and which one is an optimist.

2. Use the text to explain what emotions are and how they are produced.

3. Referring to the sidebar, explain what an MRI does and why it's used.

4. Using the sidebar that talks about evolution, explain how emotions helped human beings survive as a species.

5. According to Alan Loy McGinnis, what are three characteristics that optimists have in common?

her throughout her entire life, she'll have a hard time believing in herself. Like we said earlier, our outer environments—the people and circumstances around us—trigger our inner feelings.

But we're not completely at the mercy of outside circumstances. We also have power to choose how we respond—and how we take action. The more you understand about optimism and self-confidence, the more control you'll have over your own life.

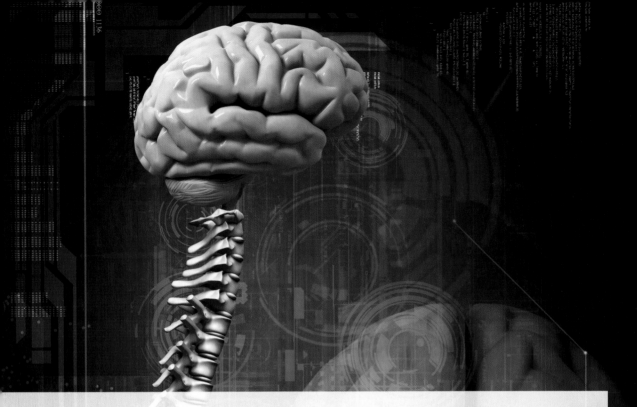

Words to Understand

genes: Pieces of DNA that contain the code for what you look like, how you feel, and everything else about your brain and body.

hormone: A chemical your body uses to send messages to certain cells.

DNA: Long chains of genes, found inside your cells. Your DNA is passed down to you from your parents.

factors: Things that affect the final result of something.

culture: All the shared thoughts, art, and ethics of a group of people.

participants: People who are involved in something.

activated: Switched on.

victim: The person something bad is done to. Victims are considered helpless—it's not their fault when something bad happens to them.

hypothesize: Make an educated guess about the result of an experiment.

strategies: Plans or ways to handle a certain situation.

TWO

What's the Connection to Your Brain & Body?

Amy and Lisa are sisters who grew up in the same home. So how come one sister looks at life so differently from the other? Scientists think that part of the answer may lie in their *genes*, the genetic material they received from their parents.

GENETICS AND OPTIMISM & SELF-CONFIDENCE

Researchers have found that a specific gene is connected to optimism and self-confidence. They've labeled that gene OXTR, because it's connected to the production of a *hormone* called oxytocin. Oxytocin is a chemical that's released in situations where human beings need a burst of positive emotion and the ability to bond with one another.

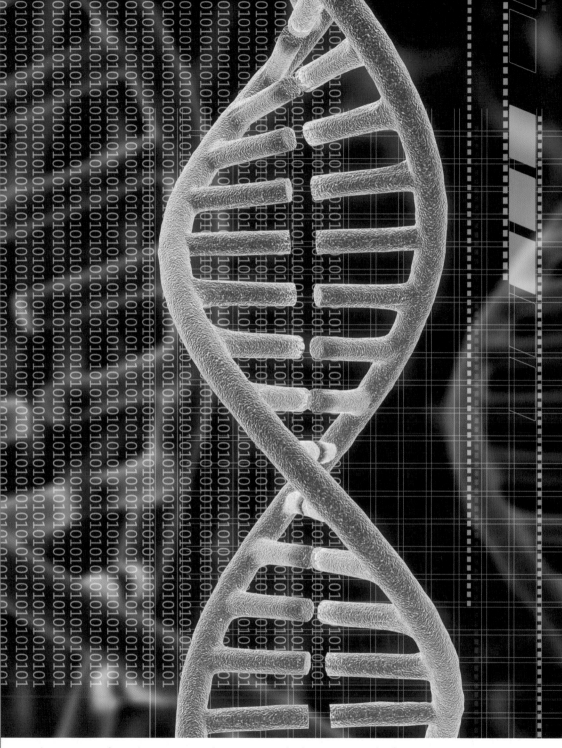

The secret of each person's identity is coded on a strand of DNA. Scientists have discovered that even qualities like optimism may be shaped by our genetic material.

The researchers studied the **DNA** of a group of people who had also completed questionnaires that measured some of their emotional traits. The researchers found that people with one kind of OXTR were more likely to be less optimistic and have lower self-confidence than people who had a different kind of OXTR. The people who were less optimistic also felt they had little power in life; they felt they had very few skills. They were also more likely to be depressed.

The scientists stressed, though, that people aren't totally at the mercy of their genes. In other words, if you have the kind of OXTR gene that's connected to less optimism and lower self-confidence, you're not necessarily doomed to a life of sadness and low achievement. One of the scientists who led the study, Dr. Shelley E. Taylor from the University of Californian in Los Angeles, said, "Some people think genes are destiny, that if you have a specific gene, then you will have a particular outcome. That is definitely not the case. This gene is one factor that influences psychological resources and depression."

She went on to say that other *factors* in your environment also play a role. The people you know, the *culture* where you grow up, the opportunities you have, and many other life circumstances will all shape who you are and how you respond to life. They will change how you respond to the world around you.

They do this by changing the way your brain acts.

BRAINS AND OPTIMISM & SELF-CONFIDENCE

A group of scientists at New York University did another study of optimism. Instead of looking at genetic makeup, this group of researchers looked at what is going on inside people's brains when they experience optimism and self-confidence.

The researchers asked people in their study to imagine positive future events. While the *participants* daydreamed, the scientists used MRIs to look inside their brains and see what was going on

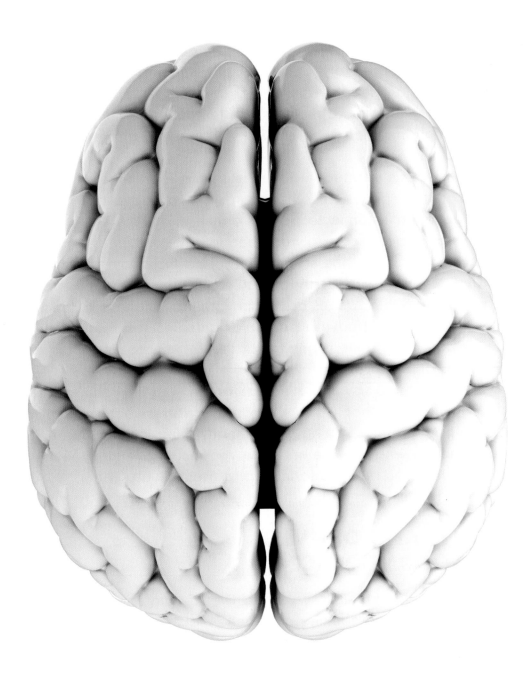

The brain's cortex is the wrinkly outer layer that makes a brain look a little a walnut.

Make Connections

Our brains are very complicated. They have many parts, and each part controls a different part of our bodies and our reactions. Usually, all the parts work together.

Two of these parts are the amygdala and the cortex. The amygdala is a small almond-shaped cluster of brain cells. The cortex is the layer of the brain often called "gray matter." Scientists sometimes say the amygdala is the emotional part of the brain, while the cortex is the rational part. The amygdala sends emotional reactions—like fear, for example—to the cortex. The cortex decides what to do about it. So say you hear the smoke alarm going off in your house. Your amygdala will send a message to your cortex: "Watch out! Something scary is going on!" The cortex then decides what to do. It sends the message to your body to get out of the building, call 911, or whatever.

there. They found that images of a happy future **activated** certain parts of the brain, parts of the cortex and the amygdala. The researchers also found that the stronger the brain response, the higher those participants scored on an optimism test.

The scientists concluded that the more optimism a person feels, the more the brain is able at the same time to downplay negative emotions. So even though the person may be disappointed by something that happens—for example, at first Lisa may have been disappointed to wake up on the day of the big game and find that the sky looked like rain—her brain is able to counteract the negative response with a positive one.

The scientists also found a connection to self-confidence. The brain's "optimism response" may also give people a drive to achieve high-stake goals. It gives them a shot of confidence. Did you ever see the old Disney movie *Dumbo*? In the movie, the little

Dumbo's "magic feather" turns him into an optimist. He flies because he thinks he can fly.

elephant with the big, floppy ears is able to fly, so long as he holds a magic feather in his trunk. In reality, of course, the feather is not what makes him able to fly at all. The feather simply gives him the confidence he needs to believe in his own abilities. That's a little like what goes on in people's brains when they imagine a positive outcome. Their brains give their self-confidence a boost.

From there it's like a snowball rolling down hill, getting bigger and faster as it goes. The more you focus on the positive, the more likely you are to take on challenges with self-confidence. The more self-confidence you have, the more likely you are to succeed (and even if you don't succeed at first, you're more likely to be able to keep trying). The more often you succeed, the more self-confidence you have in yourself, and the more optimism you feel. And of course the more optimism and self-confidence you have, the more willing you are to take on the *next* challenge. . . .

All this means that you're not just a **victim** of your genes. You're

Make Connections

 When we talk about "stress," we're referring to the feeling we get when we wonder whether we can cope with all the things life is asking us to handle. Anything that poses a challenge to our well-being can cause us stress—and even good things (getting a new pet, starting a new job, moving to a new home, or going to college, for example) can cause stress as well. Stress is an emotional reaction that was meant to prepare humans for danger. It has physical effects as well:

- Blood pressure rises.
- Breathing becomes more rapid.
- Digestive system slows down.
- Heart rate (pulse) rises.
- Immune system doesn't work as well, since the body's energy is getting ready for other dangers.
- Muscles become tense. (They're getting ready to go into action.)
- People may not be able to sleep. (The body is in a state of extra alertness.)

These physical responses are hard on the body. When people have too much stress, they are more likely to get sick.

also not a victim of your circumstances. You can choose how you think and act. And those choices will change the way your brain reacts. And the changes in your brain will make it easier for you to choose how to think and act. Scientists have proven that this is true over and over.

OPTIMISM AND SELF-CONFIDENCE

A pessimistic person might get stressed by studying for a big test, while a more optimistic person might see the same situation as far less stressful.

Make Connections

Research studies have shown that optimists have a long list of health and social benefits over the pessimist. Optimists live longer. They have better lung capacity (which means their bodies are able to take in more oxygen, allowing them to have greater physical endurance). They survive cancer treatments at a greater rate. They also have happier and longer-lasting relationships.

OPTIMISM AND STRESS

In 2013, researchers at Concordia University found a connection between stress and optimism. The scientists asked the participants in the study to rate the level of stress in their lives. Then the researchers compared participants' stress levels to how optimistic or pessimistic they were.

When we think about stress, we often believe we have little control over how much or how little of it we have in our lives. We feel as though circumstances outside our control cause our stress. If life is hard, there's really nothing we can do about it except suffer through it!

But the researchers discovered that stress actually comes from inside us as well as outside us. Joelle Jobin, one of the authors of the study, explained, "For some people, going to the grocery store on a Saturday morning can be very stressful." Jobin and the other researchers found that stress, as it turns out, is connected to optimism and pessimism.

Pessimists tend to have a higher stress level than optimists do. A pessimist could be facing exactly the same situation as an optimist—just as Lucy and Amy did in the first chapter—but a pessimist will feel that the situation is stressful, while the optimist won't. The scientists discovered that there was a physical reason for this.

Text-Dependent Questions

1. Describe the study that connected optimism to genes.

2. Using the sidebar, explain the connection between the amygdala and the cortex.

3. The author uses the elephant Dumbo as an example of how self-confidence connects to performance. Explain this connection, referring to Dumbo as an example.

4. List the eight physical effects of stress.

5. What does researcher Joelle Jobin indicate is the value of the hormone cortisol?

Pessimists generally had trouble regulating their nervous systems when they went through stressful experiences. They had high levels of a chemical called cortisol in their bodies.

When humans perceive stress in their lives, cortisol is the hormone that their bodies release. Cortisol tells the body to get ready for danger. It can be a good thing. But the body also needs to relax. When a person lives as though he's constantly ready to face a threat to his life, his body can't work the way it's meant to. His other emotions won't get triggered the way they would normally either. He's more likely to feel sad, less likely to feel happy; he's more likely to be angry, less likely to laugh.

Joelle Jobin explains, "On days where they experience higher than average stress, that's when we see that the pessimists' stress response is much elevated, and they have trouble bringing their cortisol levels back down. Optimists, by contrast, were protected in these circumstances."

Research Project

This chapter describes several research studies. Think of a question you would like to ask about optimism and self-confidence, something that isn't answered by the text in this chapter. Next, use the library and the Internet to find out how a good research study is set up. List the steps. Then create your own research study. If you can (if it doesn't take machines like MRIs or other things you don't have), find a group of volunteers (your friends or family) willing to take part in your study. See if you can find an answer to your question. If you can't actually conduct the study, make a hypothesis about what you think your study would prove if you could carry it out. Create a diagram that shows the steps you took and the answers you found.

Jobin and the other researchers found that optimists' bodies also produce cortisol—and that's a good thing, Jobin says. She says that cortisol is also the "get-up-and-get-things-done hormone." We need it to give us a kickstart and get us moving. But optimists tend to produce more cortisol in the morning, and after that, throughout the day their cortisol levels go down. The scientists *hypothesize* that optimists have learned *strategies* for focusing their attention in ways that lower their cortisol levels.

Psychologists are looking closely at findings like these. They are starting to believe that optimism and self-confidence are a complicated mixture of genetics, environment, our body's natural responses, and the choices we make as individuals. This means that you may be a "born pessimist"—but you don't have to stay that way. You can choose to become more optimistic by deciding to think and talk about the positive parts of each situation that comes along. When you do that, you change the way your body works. And you'll also change your life.

Words to Understand

social: Having to do with interactions between people.

sociologists: People who study human societies and the interactions between people.

significantly: Dramatically; in a big or important way.

discount: Ignore or consider not to be important.

incremental: In small steps.

post-traumatic stress disorder: A psychological condition where people have trouble recovering emotionally and psychologically from something bad that happened to them.

baseline: The standard level that you compare to to see if something has changed.

THREE

How Do Optimism & Self-Confidence Change Your Life?

Remember Lisa and Amy? How do you think their different outlooks affect the rest of their lives? If you had to guess, which sister do you think is most popular? Which one do you think does best in school? Notice that we're not asking which sister is smarter or more likable. Both girls may have similar skills—but their pessimism or optimism will change how they use those skills. Odds are good that Lisa, the optimist, does a little better on tests and other schoolwork because she doesn't get as nervous, which allows her to do her best. She may also do better in *social* settings, again because she's not as nervous. She can relax and just be herself, while her sister Amy, the pessimist, may be too tense to do that.

Being optimistic casts "light" over your entire life. It can allow you to see possibilities that a pessimist may miss.

Make Connections

Can you be too optimistic? Psychologists stress that healthy optimism is firmly rooted in reality. False optimism—one that's not based on reality—could lead to not preparing adequately for a task. Imagine a student who says before a final exam, "I'm so smart, I don't need to study. This is going to be easy." Confident that she's so smart, she races through the exam and turns it in before anyone else in the class. The next day when the teacher returns the graded exams, however, the student is dismayed to find a big red D on her exam paper. This person had false optimism. She wasn't merely self-confident; she was overconfident. Healthy optimism, however, is able to recognize genuine weaknesses and actual challenge. It takes control by finding realistic ways to handle challenges.

DIFFERENT EXPECTATIONS

As psychologists and *sociologists* study groups of people, they've discovered some things about optimism and pessimism. Optimists don't only expect things to turn out better, while pessimists expect disaster. The two groups of people also look differently at what *causes* the troubles in our life. Pessimists tend to take the blame for whatever happens. They tell themselves things like, "This is all *my* fault." Pessimists also tend to think that problems are so enormous that they'll change many aspects of their lives. They tell themselves, "This will change *everything*." And last, they think problems will have a permanent effect on their lives, so they think, "This can never be changed."

Lots of studies have found that these pessimistic attitudes put people at a disadvantage in life. Say you fail a test, but your teacher says that you can retake it. If you're a pessimist, you might

BOOK REPORT

Just being optimistic won't get you a good grade! If Dumbo hadn't had those enormous ears, he wouldn't have been able to fly even if he had all the self-confidence in the world. Optimism has to be rooted in reality.

tell yourself, "What's the point? I'm too stupid to understand this material. I'll just fail again." But if you're an optimist, you might say, "I know I didn't study enough the first time, but this time I will."

Psychologists have found that when pessimists fail, they tend to give up and do more poorly in the future. Martin Seligman, the psychologist who is the expert on optimism, did a study where he asked a group of swimmers to swim their best stroke—and then told them that their times were slightly slower than they actually were. When the swimmers swam the next time, the optimists in the group swam as fast or faster than they had the first time. The pessimists, however, swam more slowly.

DIFFERENT OUTCOMES

What we expect to happen can actually change the outcomes. Remember Dumbo with his magic feather? Because he expected to be able to fly, he *could* fly.

Of course, no magic feather is going to make you able to leap off from the roof of your house, flap your arms, and soar up to the clouds. That would be false optimism! No amount of confidence will change the reality that you simply lack the ability to fly.

But studies have found where we have real skills to call upon, our expectations can change how well we do. In one study, basketball players were taught to credit positive results—for example, making a free throw—to their ability, while they were instructed to blame negative results on their *lack of effort*. The players **significantly** improved their performance. Other studies with other kinds of athletes found the same results. The stories we tell ourselves about our performance change how we do in the future.

SELF-CONFIDENCE AND SUCCESS

Have you ever said something like this: "I'm terrible at math"? (Or maybe you say, "I'm terrible at gym class." Or it could be something else, from music to dating.) When you say this, you

Two people can look at the same situation—but what they see will be shaped by their individual mindsets.

Make Connections

Most people have spots in their life where they feel self-confident, and other spots where they lack confidence. For example, you may be confident of your athletic abilities, but lack confidence in your personal appearance. You probably have applied optimistic, self-confident thinking habits to one area of your life but not to others. So if you lack confidence socially but you feel pretty good about your athletic skills, what could you learn and apply from your confidence in your athletic ability? Or if you're good at schoolwork, how could you apply your attitudes toward academics to other areas of your life?

probably mean that in the past, you've not done very well in a situation that required math skills—or athletic, musical, or social skills, depending on what it is that you think you're terrible at. Your failure made you lose confidence in yourself. You'd rather label yourself as being simply "bad" at whatever it is. That way you don't have to risk trying and failing again. You believe, "I was bad at this in the past, I am bad at this now, and I will always be bad at this." You tell yourself, "I expect to fail at this because I'm bad at it, so I don't even have to try." You don't want to risk looking foolish to others.

In psychologist Carol Dweck's book *Mindset*, she describes two kinds of "mindsets."

- Self-confident people trust their own abilities. They are willing to risk others' disapproval. They accept themselves. They don't feel that they have to meet others' standards in order to prove themselves.

- People who lack self-confidence depend too much on others' approval to feel good about themselves. They tend to

OPTIMISM AND SELF-CONFIDENCE

An optimist sees this glass as half full, while the pessimist sees it as half empty. But the optimist still has a realistic mindset—he doesn't see an EMPTY glass as a full glass.

avoid risks because they fear that their failure will make them look bad to others. They often put themselves down, and they often ignore or *discount* any compliments they get.

Psychologists like Dweck have discovered that self-confidence isn't necessarily connected to actual ability. Instead, it has more to do with realistic and unrealistic expectations. If you define success as being a star athlete, for example, you may never be satisfied with any other level of athletic performance—when in fact, if you had more realistic expectations, you might be able to develop enough athletic skills that you could enjoy playing sports.

Dweck describes another two kinds of mindsets:

- A fixed mindset: the belief that talent is fixed; we are born with a certain level of ability and that our success or failure will depend on that for the rest of our lives.

- A growth/*incremental* mindset: the belief that talent is nurtured and changeable; people can develop and grow their skills.

In her book, Dweck describes many studies that demonstrate the positive effects of believing that you can improve. You may have been born with a lot of natural academic, artistic, or athletic ability—or very little. You may have grown up in a home, for example, where your parents gave you many opportunities to practice and learn academic, artistic, or athletic skills—or you may have grown up in a home with parents who had no interest in those things and did nothing to encourage you to be interested in them either. Dweck says it doesn't really matter. No matter what your level of skill is in a particular area right now, if you believe you can improve, you can! If you tell yourself, "I can get better at this if I work at it," you will.

Optimism can lead to all sorts of positive things in your life, including creativity.

Make Connections

Researchers believe that optimists are more creative than pessimists. Optimists are more likely to come up with new ideas and try new things.

RESILIENCE

Researchers have also found that optimism and self-confidence can change people's lives in another way as well. These qualities help people recover faster from the bad things that sometimes happen in life. People who are optimistic and self-confident bounce back better after a grief or loss. Psychologists call this ability "resilience."

Dr. Dennis Charney at Mount Sinai School of Medicine studied 750 Vietnam war veterans who had been prisoners of war for six to eight years. During that time, they had been tortured and kept in solitary confinement, and yet this group of men had not developed depression or *post-traumatic stress disorder* the way many other veterans do. Charney wanted to discover why this group was able to be so resilient. He found out at that all 750 men had certain qualities in common. These included a sense of humor, a reason to live, and the desire to help others. But the most important trait all the veterans shared was optimism.

Barbara Fredrickson, a psychological researcher at the University of North Carolina at Chapel Hill, has also studied the relationship between optimism and resilience. She found that having a positive mood makes people more resilient physically as well as emotionally. In other words, after a stress, the bodies of optimists bounced back to normal more quickly.

In one study, research participants were outfitted with a device that measured their heart activity. After each person's *baseline* heart rate was recorded, each participant was asked to quickly

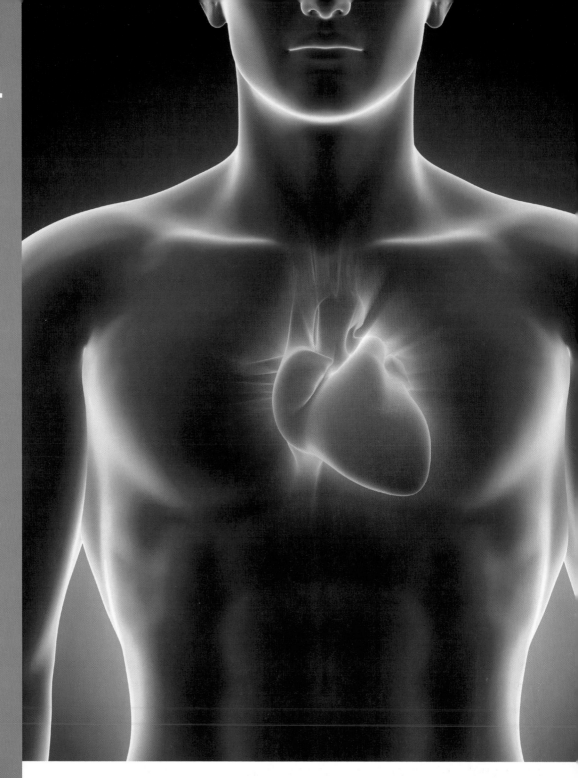

Optimism can even affect how our hearts handle stress and anxiety.

Make Connections

Studies have shown that optimism and pessimism are catching. An optimistic person can lift the confidence level of an entire group—while a pessimistic person can lower the confidence level.

prepare and give a speech. The participants were told that the speech would be videotaped and evaluated. Imagine how you would feel if you'd been given this task! The participants' heart rates shot up. So did their blood pressure. Next, the participants were told they wouldn't have to give the speech after all. Instead, they watched a short movie. One group of participants was shown a movie that made them feel sad; another group watched a movie that made them feel happy; and the third group watched a movie that wasn't designed to make them feel any emotion at all. Stress levels for all participants should have started to decrease as soon as they learned they wouldn't have to give a speech after all. The study discovered, however, that the heart rate of the group of participants who watched the happy movie returned to normal much faster than the groups who watched the other two movies. Positive feelings undo stress.

Frederickson and the other researchers in her group next tested another group of participants to see which ones were more optimistic. They again told participants they would have to give a speech and measured their heart rates and blood pressure. The researchers found that the bodies of optimistic people did not respond with as high levels of stress. When questioned, they were more likely to describe the speech as a challenge and opportunity for growth rather than as something scary and terrible. In other words, they found the silver lining in the dark cloud!

Now Frederickson and the other researchers wondered if

Text-Dependent Questions

1. Describe three ways that pessimists think about problems.

2. Explain how "false optimism" is different from healthy optimism.

3. Explain the concept of resilience and why it's related to optimism.

4. The text states, "Positive feelings undo stress." Describe the research study that indicates this statement is true.

5. Explain how Barbara Frederickson's research indicates that people can learn to be more optimistic.

people could be taught to be more resilient by helping them be more optimistic. This time, the researchers gave the participants the same task—having to give a speech—but they told one group to see the task as an exciting challenge, while they told the other group to look at the task as something scary and threatening. Here's what they found: Resilient, optimistic people who saw the task as a challenge did fine, as predicted. So did resilient, optimistic people who were told to view the task as a threat. Resilient, optimistic people, no matter how they approached the task, had the same heartbeat recovery rate. But the pessimists in both groups were the ones who changed. Those who were told to approach the task as an exciting opportunity rather than a threat suddenly started looking like the resilient people. They bounced back quicker. Their heart rates slowed down more quickly.

Frederickson stresses that optimists aren't simply happy and calm no matter what happens. Their heart rates and blood

Research Project

Using the information provided so far in this book, design a questionnaire to "test" how pessimistic or optimistic people are. Your questionnaire should have 20 questions, each one connected in some way to the research-based characteristics of optimists and pessimists. Find volunteers among your friends and family to take the test. When you show them the results of your test, explain to them the ways that being more optimistic helps people. Write a paragraph to describe how people react to the knowing whether they are optimists or pessimists. Include how open the participants in your test were to new ideas about optimism and pessimism. Did you find that the pessimists were less open to new ideas than the optimists were? If so, how does this connect to the information given in this chapter?

pressure go up when they're faced with challenges. But they let go of their fears more quickly. They shift their attention to positive things more easily. They're open to thinking about new things. They bounce back to normal faster.

So here's the message: optimism and self-confidence can change your life. They can make you more successful, and they can make you handle problems better. And the best news of all? These qualities can be learned.

Words to Understand

arousal: A feeling of being excited or stimulated.
assure: Make sure something happens.
habitual: Done constantly; the way you're used to doing things.

FOUR

What Can You Learn?

Most of us are optimists sometimes and pessimists sometimes. Sometimes we react like Amy, and sometimes we're more like Lisa. But we usually have a general, overall approach to life.

Optimism is more than an emotion we feel now and then. It's an outlook on life. If we're optimists, we're not always happy and laughing. But we do tend to be more upbeat and positive. We don't give up when hard times come. We have enough confidence in ourselves that we keep trying even when we make mistakes. We believe our actions matter. No matter how hard something is, we know there's always something we can do to make it better. And optimism itself is one of those things we can get better at!

Dr. Jason Selk is a coach for individuals, businesses, and professional athletes and their coaches. He offers eight ways you can train yourself to be more optimistic.

Unfortunately, there's no magic optimism drink you can gulp down. But you can create more optimistic thinking habits.

1. Look for solutions rather than problems.

Whenever you catch yourself focusing on a problem or doubting yourself, ask yourself this question: "What's one thing I can do differently that could make this situation better?" This technique replaces a problem-focused thought with solution-focused thinking. It gives you hope. It builds both optimism and self-confidence.

2. Create an upbeat "movie" of your life.

Take a few minutes to imagine a short YouTube video of your ideal life. Include specific details about how you look, how you feel, where you live, what you're doing, what you've accomplished, and what your life is like. Take 30 seconds every day to play this video in your mind. Dr. Selk suggests setting an alarm on your phone to remind yourself to replay this mental video each day at the same time. It may sound silly, but it's a simple mental training exercise that's been proven to lift your mood and change the way you think about yourself.

3. Acknowledge any improvement to the current situation.

All of us want to find "big answers." We want to fix everything permanently. But life isn't like that. Big successes don't happen without lots of small, in-between steps along the way. Get into the habit of looking for any small improvement in the current situation, and then allow it to encourage you.

4. Keep performance arousal at a moderate level.

"Performance *arousal*" is that pumped-up feeling that comes when you're faced with a challenge. You'll do better if you can stay calm and self-confident. Preparing ahead of time is the best way to do this.

5. Keep a coach inside your head.

Many of us feel more confident and perform better when we know someone is cheering us on. At the same time, we need to be able to be in touch with reality, so that we can take action in the right ways to *assure* our success. So imagine a coach in your mind who gives you advice while encouraging you. This could be a real person who has inspired and challenged you, or it could be

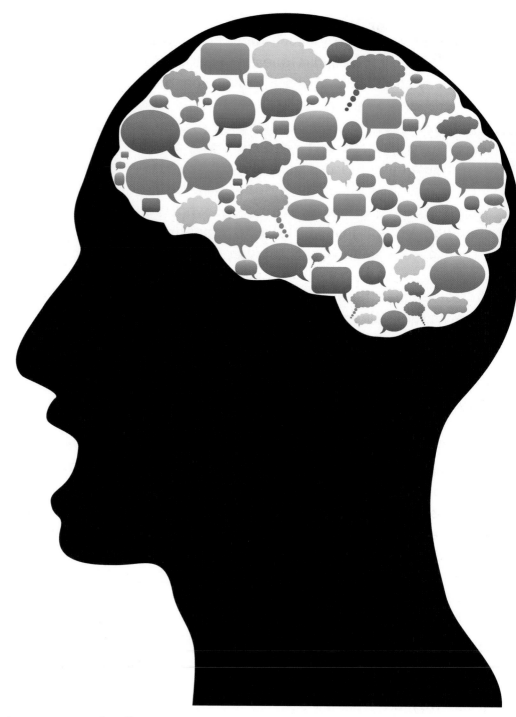

We are constantly talking to ourselves with our thoughts. We can't stop the chatter inside our heads—but we can teach ourselves to have more positive self-talk.

Make Connections

Psychologists refer to the running stream of thoughts that goes on inside our heads as "self-talk." Most of this goes on without us ever noticing. Use your emotions as triggers for noticing your self-talk. The next time you feel happy, for example, pay attention to your thoughts. They're probably pretty positive. But if you notice yourself feeling sad and discouraged, your self-talk is likely much more negative. As you learn to pay attention and catch your self-talk in action, you'll be able to replace negative self-talk with positive. You'll be able to rewrite the script that's playing inside your head. Psychologists say this is a powerful technique for changing your life.

a person from a movie you've watched or a book you've read. Then, the next time you're faced with a challenge, ask yourself, "What would this person tell me?"

6. Minimize distractions to success.

All of us get discouraged when life seems to be coming at us from a million different directions at once. You'll do better if you deal with just one thing at a time. If you're studying for a test, don't try to text your friend at the same time. Do what you need to do to ensure success in a particular area—and then set it aside and move on to something else.

7. Be happy from the inside out.

Feeling optimistic and self-confident is easier when you feel healthy. Lack of sleep, poor eating habits, and too little exercise can all interfere with your emotional and physical energy levels. If you have a big goal to achieve, you might want to "train" for it the way an athlete trains for the Olympics or some other big event. Sleep, rest, a good diet, and exercise are all part of successful training.

Nope, there's no magic pill for optimism either! But you can change your outlook by changing your thoughts.

Psychologists have found that when optimists are criticized, they are more able to accept the criticism and use it to grow than pessimists can.

8. Allow yourself "well dones."

Give yourself a pat on the back. Take a few seconds every day to ask the question, "What have I done well today?" This daily habit builds optimism and self-confidence.

Experts like Dr. Selk have found that optimistic people with self-confidence make a habit of thinking certain things. And the same is true for pessimists. So we can choose which one we want to be.

PESSIMISTIC VS. OPTIMISTIC THOUGHTS

Here are some of the *habitual* thoughts that pessimistic people think, followed by a more optimistic, self-confident thought.

Pessimistic: "I need everyone in my life to love and approve of me."

Optimistic: "Not everyone is ever going to approve of everything I do. I care more that I do the best I can at the things that are most important to me."

Pessimistic: "I need to do well at every area of my life. I have to make major achievements in every area. If I don't, then I feel like failure."

Optimistic: "I am always going to be better at some things than others. I can choose to work hard and do better—but my personal worth doesn't change whether I'm good or bad at something."

WELCOME TO

OPTIMISM

ENJOY THE JOURNEY

Who knows what you can accomplish in life? Believe in the possibilities!

Make Connections

The University of Illinois offers these techniques for building your self-confidence:

Emphasize Strengths. Give yourself credit for everything you try. By focusing on what you can do, you applaud yourself for efforts rather than emphasizing end products. Starting from a base of what you should do helps you live within the bounds of your inevitable limitations.

Take Risks. Approach new experiences as opportunities to learn rather than occasions to win or lose. Doing so opens you up to new possibilities and can increase your sense of self-acceptance. Not doing so turns every possibility into an opportunity for failure, and inhibits personal growth.

Self-Evaluate. Learn to evaluate yourself independently. Doing so allows you to avoid the constant sense of turmoil that comes from relying exclusively on the opinions of others. Focusing internally on how you feel about your own behavior, work, etc. will give you a stronger sense of self and will prevent you from giving your personal power away to others.

(Adapted from:
www.counselingcenter.illinois.edu/self-help-brochures/
self-awarenessself-care/self-confidence)

Pessimistic: "The past controls the present and the future. If I was bad at something or made mistakes in the past, I probably will whenever I try to do that thing again."

Optimistic: "I can change and grow. I can get better at the things that are important to me. I don't have to ever stop improving."

Text-Dependent Questions

1. The second paragraph of this chapter gives five qualities of an optimist. Can you list them?

2. Give a definition of "performance arousal" and explain why too much of it is not a good thing.

3. Explain what self-talk is and how it relates to optimism and self-confidence.

4. Give an example of a pessimistic thought and the optimistic thought to replace it.

5. List the three strategies for developing self-confidence offered by the University of Illinois.

Pessimistic: "Whenever my performance is not perfect, I am a total failure."
Optimistic: "I messed up this time, but I can learn from my failure so that I'll do better next time."

Pessimistic: "Disaster and failure are everywhere."
Optimistic: "The world is full of possibility and opportunities."

Pessimistic: "Good events don't count as much as bad events."
Optimistic: "Setbacks are one-time things. They're only temporary."

Pessimistic: "Emotions are true. If I'm in a bad mood, reality must also be bad."
Optimistic: "Emotions come and go. I may be in a bad mood today, but things will look better tomorrow."

Research Project

Think of a fiction book you have read recently. Examine two of the main characters and determine whether they are pessimists or optimists, based on their dialogue and how the author describes them. Give evidence from the story to support your conclusion and describe how the characters' outlook shapes their lives.

Pessimistic: "Negative labels (like 'loser') describe me."
Optimistic: "No negative label describes me. I am bigger than my actions. I may make mistakes, but overall, I am a winner."

Pessimistic: "The compliments I receive aren't true."
Optimistic: "Compliments help me to see my strengths more clearly."

Pay attention to your thoughts and words. The next time you catch yourself thinking or saying something similar to the pessimistic statements above, reframe the thought. Make it optimistic. When you do, you'll be on the road toward new thinking habits. The more you think optimistic thoughts, the more you'll retrain your brain. Your optimism will grow. So will your self-confidence.

Find Out More

IN BOOKS

Fox, Marci. *Think Confident, Be Confident for Teens.* Oakland, Calif.: Instant Help, 2011.

Rutherford, David. *Navy SEAL Training: Self-Confidence.* New York: Leading Line, 2012.

Seligman, Martin. *Learned Optimism: How to Change Your Mind and Life.* New York: Vintage, 2006.

ONLINE

Positive Thinking for Kids
positivethinkingforkids.com

63 Ways to Build Self-Confidence
www.lifehack.org/articles/lifehack/63-ways-to-build-self-confidence.html

The Story on Self-Esteem
kidshealth.org/kid/feeling/emotion/self_esteem.html

Series Glossary of Key Terms

adrenaline: An important body chemical that helps prepare your body for danger. Too much adrenaline can also cause stress and anxiety.

amygdala: An almond-shaped area within the brain where the flight-or-flight response takes place.

autonomic nervous system: The part of your nervous system that works without your conscious control, regulating body functions such as heartbeat, breathing, and digestion.

cognitive: Having to do with thinking and conscious mental activities.

cortex: The area of your brain where rational thinking takes place.

dopamine: A brain chemical that gives pleasure as a reward for certain activities.

endorphins: Brain chemicals that create feelings of happiness.

fight-or-flight response: Your brain's reaction to danger, which sends out messages to the rest of the body, getting it ready to either run away or fight.

hippocampus: Part of the brain's limbic system that plays an important role in memory.

hypothalamus: The brain structure that gets messages out to your body's autonomic nervous system, preparing it to face danger.

limbic system: The part of the brain where emotions are processed.

neurons: Nerve cells found in the brain, spinal cord, and throughout the body.

neurotransmitters: Chemicals that carry messages across the tiny gaps between nerve cells.

serotonin: A neurotransmitter that plays a role in happiness and depression.

stress: This feeling that life is just too much to handle can be triggered by anything that poses a threat to our well-being, including emotions, external events, and physical illnesses.

Index

63

About the Author & Consultant

Z.B. Hill is an author and publicist living in Binghamton, NY. He has a special interest in adolescent education.

Cindy Croft is director of the Center for Inclusive Child Care at Concordia University, St. Paul, Minnesota where she also serves as faculty in the College of Education. She is field faculty at the University of Minnesota Center for Early Education and Development program and teaches for the Minnesota on-line Eager To Learn program. She has her M.A. in education with early childhood emphasis. She has authored *The Six Keys: Strategies for Promoting Children's Mental Health in Early Childhood Programs* and co-authored *Children and Challenging Behavior: Making Inclusion Work* with Deborah Hewitt. She has worked in the early childhood field for the past twenty years.

Picture Credits

Fotolia.com:
8: kikkerdirk
10: Stuart Miles
12: James Steidl
14: WavebreakmediaMicro
16: photo 5000
20: adimas
22: abhijith3747
24: vasabii
28: amyinlondon
32: dampoint
34: alexcoolok
38: jojje11

40: Andrzej Wilusz
42: Welf Aaron
44: CLIPAREA.com
48: pathdoc
50: mik38
52: HuHu Lin
54: Pixelbliss
56: creative soul

26: Walt Disney
36: Christopher Sista | Dreamstime.com

BOOK CHARGING CARD

Accession No. _____ Call No. _____

Author _____

Title _____

Date Loaned	Borrower's Name	Date Returned